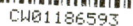

THE FORES
COMPTON
HORSHAM
TEL: (01403) 261086/7

This book is due for return on or before the last date shown below.

The Spirals Series

Fiction

Jim Alderson
The Witch Princess

Jan Carew
Death Comes to the Circus
Footprints in the Sand
Voices in the Dark

Barbara Catchpole
Laura Called
Nick

Susan Duberley
The Ring

Keith Fletcher and Susan Duberley
Nightmare Lake

John Goodwin
Dead-end Job
Ghost Train

Angela Griffiths
Diary of a Wild Thing

Marian Iseard
Loved to Death

Anita Jackson
The Actor
The Austin Seven
Bennet Manor
Dreams
The Ear
A Game of Life and Death
No Rent to Pay

Paul Jennings
Eye of Evil
Maggot

Helen Lowerson
The Biz

Margaret Loxton
The Dark Shadow

Patrick Nobes
Ghost Writer

David Orme
City of the Roborgs
The Haunted Asteroids

Kevin Philbin
Summer of the Werewolf

Bill Ridgway
Jack's Video
Mr Punch

Julie Taylor
Spiders

John Townsend
Back on the Prowl
Beware the Morris Minor
Fame and Fortune
Night Beast
A Minute to Kill
Snow Beast

Non-fiction

Jim Alderson
Crash in the Jungle

David Orme
Hackers

Bill Ridgway
Lost in Alaska

Julie Taylor
Lucky Dip

John Townsend
Burke and Hare: The Body Snatchers
SOS

Plays

Jan Carew
Computer Killer
No Entry

Julia Donaldson
Books and Crooks

John Godfrey
When I Count to Three

Angela Griffiths
Wally and Co

Paul Groves
Tell Me Where it Hurts

Barbara Mitchelhill
Punchlines
The Ramsbottoms at Home

Bill Ridgway
Monkey Business

John Townsend
A Bit of a Shambles
Breaking the Ice
Cheer and Groan
Clogging the Works
Cowboys, Jelly and Custard
Hanging by a Fred
Hiccups and Slip-ups
Jumping the Gun
The Lighthouse Keeper's Secret
A Lot of Old Codswallop
Making a Splash
Over and Out
Rocking the Boat
Spilling the Beans
Taking the Plunge

David Walke
The Good, the Bad and the Bungle
Package Holiday

NEW Spirals
PLAYS

Wally and Co

Angela Griffiths

Text © Angela Griffiths 2001

The right of Angela Griffiths to be identified as author of this work has been asserted by her in accordance with the Copyright, Designs and Patents Act 1988.

All rights reserved. No part of this publication may be reproduced or transmitted in any form or by any means, electronic or mechanical, including photocopy, recording or any information storage and retrieval system, without permission in writing from the publisher or under licence from the Copyright Licensing Agency Limited. Further details of such licences (for reprographic reproduction) may be obtained from the Copyright Licensing Agency Limited, 90 Tottenham Court Road, London W1T 4LP.

First published in 2001 by:
Nelson Thornes Ltd
Delta Place
27 Bath Road
CHELTENHAM
GL53 7TH
United Kingdom

01 02 03 04 05 / 10 9 8 7 6 5 4 3 2 1

A catalogue record for this book is available from the British Library.

ISBN 0-7487-6066-0

Cover artwork by Harry Venning
Typeset by Tech-Set, Gateshead
Printed and bound in Great Britain by Martins The Printers Ltd, Berwick upon Tweed

Contents

Five short plays, each for four parts.

Wally and Co: Window Cleaners _____ 6
4 parts: Wally
          Wayne
          Justin
          Woman

Wally and Co: Kitchen Fitters _____ 15
4 parts: Wally
          Wayne
          Mr Crick
          Mrs Crick

Wally and Co: House Painters _____ 21
4 parts: Wally
          Wayne
          Lord Nibs
          Lady Nibs

Wally and Co: Loft Laggers _____ 27
4 parts: Wally
          Wayne
          Lara
          Ash

Wally and Co: Garden Fixers _____ 34
4 parts: Wally
          Wayne
          Hector
          Posy

Wally and Co: Window Cleaners

4 parts: Wally
          Wayne
          Justin
          Woman

Scene: Wally and Wayne are unpacking their van outside a large house.

Wally	Our first job as window cleaners. This is a big moment, Wayne.
Wayne	Yes. A big moment, Wally.
Wally	But we can make it a quick job. I made the woman pay us first.
Wayne	Wise move, Wally.
Wally	We have to stay ahead!
Wayne	I'm just a bit worried.
Wally	Worried?
Wayne	Yes. I don't like the look of that big dog over there on the lawn. He keeps watching me.
Wally	He's a watchdog. He won't hurt you.

Wayne	And what about these ladders? Lots of the rungs are missing.
Wally	Don't fuss. I haven't had time to mend them yet. Just mind where you put your feet.
Wayne	And these red buckets with 'FIRE' written on them. They are so heavy. Where did you get them?
Wally	Oh, I picked them up somewhere. They were just hanging around. Not being used. Some fool had filled them with sand.
Wayne	[*Looking up at the house*] We won't have to clean those high attic windows, will we?
Wally	No problem. I've made a cradle – like the ones used on high office buildings.
Wayne	Really?
Wally	Yes. It didn't cost much. I used a plank of wood, some old rope and a couple of pulleys. It's all ready to go. And Wayne, guess what?
Wayne	What?
Wally	YOU can be first to try it out!
Wayne	No!
Wally	Yes! I knew you'd be dying to have a go. But don't worry yet. First we'll clean the windows on the middle floor. Start filling the buckets from that hose over there.

[A young boy arrives on a skateboard]

Justin	Hello. I'm Justin.
Wayne	Just in time! Ha!
Wally	I wouldn't hang around here with that skateboard if I were you. We're busy. You could get in our way.
Wayne	Not only that. You wouldn't want to meet the woman who lives here! She's built like a sumo wrestler!
Justin	Excuse me, but –
Wally	And she's got a voice like a sergeant major.
Justin	But –
Wayne	Put it this way. If you met her in a dark alley, you'd run a mile!
Justin	You happen to be talking about my mother!
Wayne	Oh! Sorry. We didn't know you lived here.
Wally	Well, Justin, we think you'd better take your skateboard to the other end of the drive. That way you won't get in our way – and we won't get in your way. Now, do you see it my way?
Justin	Yes. Okay. I'll go. See you later.

[Justin goes off on his skateboard. Wally and Wayne climb their ladders and start cleaning the middle-floor windows]

Wayne	Hey, this is good fun. I like sloshing water about.
Wally	It's fun looking through the windows. I can see a four-poster bed through mine. What can you see?
Wayne	Hold on, it's a bit steamy. I can see soap and towels . . . a Mickey Mouse toothbrush . . . some false teeth in a glass . . . a long white bath . . . and . . . OH NO!
Wally	What!
Wayne	Someone is in the bath!
Wally	Who?
Wayne	How do I know?

[*The window opens*]

Woman	How dare you! How dare you!
Wayne	I'm sorry. I didn't know. I didn't mean to . . .
Woman	You peeping Tom! You perfect pest!
Wayne	But, but . . .
Woman	You rat! You snake! You skunk! You sleazy slug!

[*The window slams shut*]

Wally	I don't think she likes you, Wayne.
Wayne	I'm going down.

Wally	Mind the gap!
Wayne	[*Falling*] AAAAAARRGGHH!
Wally	Lucky you landed in a rose bush.
Wayne	Yes, lucky!
Wally	Do you need any help?
Wayne	Yes! Come and drag this hairy hound off me.
Wally	Is he biting you?
Wayne	No, but he's having a taste!

[*Wally climbs down his ladder and helps Wayne to get free of the dog*]

Wally	Right, let's do the attic windows next. We can try out the cradle.
Wayne	We?
Wally	Yes. You can go up on it. I'll stay on the ground and work the pulleys.
Wayne	I've lost something.
Wally	What have you lost?
Wayne	My nerve!
Wally	Trust me. Go on, grab your sponge and hop on. Now I'll pull you up.

[*Creak . . . creak . . . creak*]

Wayne	Oh. I don't like this.
Wally	Up and away!

Wayne	Oooh, I feel scared.
Wally	Don't fuss, Wayne. Nothing can go wrong. It took me ten solid minutes to make that cradle.
Wayne	Wally! The rope is rotten! It's about to snap!
Wally	What? I can't hear you.
Wayne	The rope! It's making a funny noise. Like ping, ping, ping!
Wally	What? What? What?
Wayne	Help! Help! Help! The board is tipping! I'm sliding off! [*Falling*] AAAAAARRGGHH!
Wally	It was lucky you landed on the dog.
Wayne	Not so lucky for the dog!

[*Woman rushes out of the house*]

Woman	What has happened to my dog? Why is he lying there like that?
Wally	He's resting.
Wayne	Flat out.
Woman	Oh, my darling Poochie! Speak to Mumsie! Give me a sign. A little bark. A woof. A twitch of a whisker. Anything. [*Pause*] Oh dear, he's so still.
Wally	Still sleeping.
Wayne	He's dog-tired.

Woman	Where's my son? [*Calls out*] Justin! Justin! Come here. Quickly! We have a crisis! A dog crisis!

[*Justin zooms in on his skateboard*]

Justin	Don't worry, Mum. I know just what to do. I saw a film about it. You have to get close and whisper up the dog's nostrils.
Woman	Are you sure? I thought that film was about horses, not dogs.
Justin	Same thing. They've both got a leg at each corner. Watch this.

[*Justin bends down and whispers to the dog. The dog suddenly jumps up*]

Woman	How amazing! Is Poochie all right?
Justin	Yes. He's just a bit warm.
Wally	A hot dog!
Justin	Mum, am I a clever boy? Am I? Am I? Am I?
Woman	Yes, Justin. You're a wizard. Come on, let's go into the house. You can have a big bar of chocolate – and Poochie can have a big steak!

[*The woman goes indoors with Justin and the dog*]

Wally	I think it's time we left. Start packing the stuff into the van, Wayne.

Wayne	No sooner said than done!
Wally	Watch that ladder. Don't swing it round like that. There could be a nasty . . . [*Sound of breaking glass*] . . . accident.
Wayne	OOPS!
Wally	And watch out, Wayne! Mind! You're going to step on that . . .
Wayne	Oh!
Wally	. . . skateboard.
Wayne	Hey! Why has it gone dark all of a sudden? Why does my voice sound funny? Why? Why? Why?
Wally	You've got your head stuck in a bucket, that's why. Hold on. I'll pull it off.
Wayne	OUCH! OUCH!
Wally	Oh dear. You've got a problem, Wayne. In fact you've got two problems.
Wayne	What do you mean?
Wally	It's your big ears. The bucket just won't budge.
Wayne	Oooh . . . oooh.
Wally	Cheer up. I'll tap a little tune on the side of the bucket, if you like.
Wayne	Oooh. I'm feeling a little pale.

Wally   Come on. I'll drive you to hospital. It's lucky for you that I'm here.

Wayne   Yes. Very lucky.

Wally   Well, we're in this together. After all, you could say, we're lucky Wally and Co!

Wally and Co: Kitchen Fitters

4 parts: Wally
          Wayne
          Mr Crick
          Mrs Crick

Scene: Mr and Mrs Crick's new kitchen.

Wally	It won't take us long to put up a wall cupboard. We could be home by noon.
Wayne	Don't be so sure. I've spent ten minutes trying to get this flat-pack open!
Wally	Mind out. I'll jump on it. There, that's open.
Wayne	[*Unpacking*] There are lots of parts. Here's the instruction sheet. I bet you'll have a job to read it.
Wally	Why?
Wayne	It's written in Chinese.
Wally	Turn it over. English is on the other side. Let's see what it says. Slot A into B . . .
Wayne	Then slot B into C . . .
Wally	Then hammer AA into BB . . .

15

Wayne	And follow through with CC and DD.
Wally	Wayne, why are you reading the back of the sheet?
Wayne	It's easier in Chinese.
Wally	There. That's it then. It's all put together.
Wayne	It didn't take long, did it?
Wally	Simple. No sweat.

[*Mr and Mrs Crick enter the kitchen*]

Mr Crick	How's it going?
Wally	Fine.
Wayne	We're just about to fix the cupboard to the wall.
Mr Crick	Make sure it's low – so that I can reach it.
Mrs Crick	But not too low – in case I bump my head.
Mr Crick	And make sure it's level.
Mrs Crick	It must be level.
Mr Crick	And make sure it's firmly fixed.
Mrs Crick	Fix it as firm as a rock.
Wally	Don't worry, Mrs Crick. You run along now. Leave it to the experts.
Wayne	What experts? Oh, I see. Yes, just leave it to us.

[*Mr and Mrs Crick leave the kitchen*]

Wally	Right, Wayne. Lift the cupboard up to the wall. I want to put marks where I have to drill.

Wayne	Right. [*Straining to lift the cupboard*] Oooh, it's heavy.
Wally	Up a bit.
Wayne	Hurry. My arms are hurting.
Wally	Down a bit.
Wayne	Ow! Ow!
Wally	Left a bit.
Wayne	My arms are about to give way. [*The cupboard falls*] AAAAAARRGGHH!
Wally	It's a good thing the cupboard didn't break. Lucky it landed on your head.
Wayne	Yes, lucky!
Wally	Now I'll start drilling the wall. [*Drilling sounds*] There, that's the first hole done.
Wayne	Wally, I think I can smell gas.
Wally	Don't be daft! [*Sniffs*] Oh dear, you could be right. See that cat's food dish over there on the floor? Hand it up to me. Quick.
Wayne	Why? Are you hungry?
Wally	Don't be daft! I want to use the mushy food to plug the hole.
Wayne	Oh. I see. I wish I had your brains.
Wally	Now I'll drill the second hole. [*Drilling sounds*] OH NO!

[*Water gushes out of the wall*]

Wayne	Here, have my chewing gum!
Wally	Thanks – but I'd rather have a fresh bit.
Wayne	No, I mean we can plug the hole with it. [*He pushes it into the hole*] Clever or what?
Wally	Now for the third hole. [*Drilling sounds*] There. Third time lucky.
Wayne	Wally, can I drill the last hole?
Wally	Sure.
Wayne	I've always wanted to use a power drill. [*Drilling sounds*] AAAAAARRGGHH! [*He falls to the floor*]
Wally	Oh no! He's drilled through an electric cable! Wayne! Wayne! Speak to me! Wake up!

[*Mr and Mrs Crick rush into the kitchen*]

Mr Crick	We heard a scream.
Mrs Crick	What's going on?
Mr Crick	Look! There on the floor!
Mrs Crick	A body! Or is he just asleep?
Wally	He's had a shock. The electric kind.
Mr Crick	Well, it's lucky for him that we go to First Aid classes.
Mrs Crick	Yes. We know what to do. The kiss of life. It's on page seven of our First Aid book.

Mr Crick	But we're only up to page three. Oh, go on then, dear. Try it out.
Mrs Crick	Right! I will!
Wayne	[*Jumping up fast*] No way! I feel better now. Fit as a fiddle. Right as rain.
Mr Crick	[*Sniffs*] I think I can smell gas.
Mrs Crick	[*Sniffs*] Yes, I can smell it too.
Wally	All new kitchens smell of gas. It's natural.
Wayne	Natural gas.
Mr Crick	We'd better phone the Gas Company.
Mrs Crick	Let's do it now!

[*Mr and Mrs Crick rush away*]

Wally	I think we should leave. Right now. Put our stuff in the van, Wayne. Hurry! Why are you so slow?
Wayne	I'm saving energy.

[*Wally and Wayne pack the van*]

Wally	Where's my blow lamp? Is it still in the kitchen?
Wayne	Yes. Sorry. I forgot to pick it up.
Wally	I hope you remembered to put the flame out.
Wayne	Oh. It won't do any harm, will it?

[*BANG!*]

Wally   I think it just has!

Wayne   It's lucky we're here and not there.

Wally   That's us. Lucky Wally and Co!

Wally and Co: House Painters

4 parts: Wally
Wayne
Lord Nibs
Lady Nibs

Scene: Outside Bodkin Manor.

Wally   Right. Have you finished unpacking the van?

Wayne   Yes, Wally. Paint . . . ladders . . . scaffolding . . .

Wally   [*Looking up at the house*] Big place, isn't it. We were lucky to get this job.

Wayne   And we were lucky to get that paint so cheap before the shop closed down.

Wally   Fifty litres of Sludge Green and fifty litres of Sizzling Pink.

Wayne   Nice paint, shame about the colours.

Wally   Ssh! Keep your voice down!

[*Lord and Lady Nibs arrive*]

Lord Nibs   Good morning, men. I see you're keen to start work.

Wally	Ever so keen.
Lady Nibs	What colour paint did you choose? Go on, surprise me.
Wally	Well, we chose an interesting shade of green . . .
Wayne	. . . and an unusual shade of pink.
Lady Nibs	Mmmm. That is a surprise.
Wally	Those colours are very popular.
Wayne	There's none left in the shops.
Lord Nibs	Really? How lucky. Well, enjoy your work. [*To Lady Nibs*] Come on, my dear, let's go in and finish our game of Ludo.

[*Lord and Lady Nibs go into the house*]

Wally	Right. Let's put up the scaffolding.

[*Lots of banging*]

Wayne	That didn't take long. I hope it's safe.
Wally	Safe as houses. Grab your paint. We're going up in the world.
Wayne	Don't look down.
Wally	I never do. I just paint with my eyes shut.
Wayne	Just slap it on, eh?
Wally	Yes. We've got loads of paint.
Wayne	Well, I reckon we've made a good job of these window frames. They look nice!

Wally	Wayne, don't step back to admire your work!
Wayne	[*Going down*] Yeeeeeeeeeaaaaaah! [*Coming up*] Yeeeeeeeeeaaaaaah!
Wally	Lucky for you that your braces got caught on a hook.
Wayne	Yes, lucky!
Wally	How does it feel to be a bungee jumper?
Wayne	[*Bouncing up and down*] It feels . . . really scary . . . I hate . . . going up . . . and down . . . and up . . . and down . . . like this. Help me!
Wally	Hang about. I'll cut your braces.
Wayne	[*Falls to the ground*] OUCH!
Wally	Lucky you were near the ground.
Wayne	Pah!
Wally	We'll paint the front door next. I'll open the other tin of paint.
Wayne	I'm looking forward to sloshing about with that Sizzling Pink. I think I must have a hidden artistic streak.
Wally	It's not so hidden. You've got paint all over you.
Wayne	I can wash it off.
Wally	Where?
Wayne	There's lots of water over there. Very handy. I washed out some paint tins in it.

Wally	Wayne! That is a fish pond!
Wayne	Oh dear.

[*Wally and Wayne rush to the pond*]

Wally	Look at the fish! They're not a bit happy – they all look down in the mouth! They're very still.
Wayne	They do look a bit off-colour. What shall we do?
Wally	We'll carry on as if nothing has happened. Come on. Let's get busy painting again.
Wayne	I suppose you're in a bad mood now, Wally.
Wally	Well, yes. Just a bit.
Wayne	I'll cheer you up with a joke. What do you get if you cross a fish with an elephant?
Wally	I don't know. What do you get if you cross a fish with an elephant?
Wayne	Long grey swimming trunks!
Wally	Ha very ha!

[*Lord and Lady Nibs arrive*]

Lord Nibs	Hello, men. We saw you through the window. You were looking at our prize fish.
Wally	Prize fish?
Lady Nibs	Yes. Koi carp. We are going to sell them soon.
Lord Nibs	The money will help to pay for a new roof. The fish are worth an awful lot of money.

Wayne	What sort of an awful lot of money?
Lady Nibs	Each fish is worth about a thousand pounds.
Wally	No!
Lord Nibs	Yes. Come to the pond. I'll show you. Each fish is different.
Wayne	Very different.
Wally	We can't stop work now. Our brushes will dry out. We'll have to see the fish another time.
Lady Nibs	[*To Lord Nibs*] Nibsie, dear, let's go and get the prize cups we've won for Best Koi Carp. I'm sure the men would like to see them.
Lord Nibs	Good idea! We'll dust the cups and bring them out.

[*Lord and Lady Nibs rush away*]

Wally	Wayne, pack our stuff into the van. Be quick!
Wayne	[*Carrying a tin of paint*] I'm trying to be quick. But I'm having a bit of bother.
Wally	Hurry!
Wayne	Oops! I've spilled a bit of paint.
Wally	More than a bit!
Wayne	The path looks nice with pink and green stripes.
Wally	Come on, Wayne. Why are you so slow?
Wayne	I can't help being slow. It's your fault.

Wally　　Why is it my fault?

Wayne　　You cut my braces.

[*Wally and Wayne drive off and are soon a long way from Bodkin Manor*]

Wally　　[*Driving*] I've gone right off my supper now.

Wayne　　Why is that?

Wally　　I was planning to have fish and chips.

Wayne　　You mustn't get upset about a few fish.

Wally　　I'm not. It's the mushy peas I can't face. And the strawberry yoghurt.

Wayne　　I see what you mean. Same colour as the paint.

Wally　　It's lucky that I've got a big bag of crisps in the van.

Wayne　　Yes, very lucky.

Wally　　Well, that's us, isn't it. Lucky Wally and Co!

Wally and Co: Loft Laggers

4 parts: Wally
Wayne
Lara
Ash

Scene: The top floor of a tall house. Wally and Wayne are about to go up into the loft.

Wally	Six floors up. All those stairs! I'm worn out before we start!
Wayne	What about me? I had to carry all the heavy stuff.
Wally	Let's check that we've got everything we need.
Wayne	Right. I've got five rolls of glass fibre blanket and the heavy-duty vacuum cleaner.
Wally	And I've got the scissors. That's it then. Now we can climb up the ladder into the loft.

[*Two young people arrive*]

Lara	Hi! I'm Lara.
Ash	And I'm Ash.
Lara	We live here. There are ten bedsits.

Ash	All full of medical students. We're training at the hospital up the road.
Wally	If we get taken ill, we'll be sure to call you.
Wayne	Is there a doctor in the house? Ha!
Lara	What are you going to do in the loft?
Wally	Your landlord wants us to lag it. We have to lay rolls of glass fibre.
Lara	This house needs a lot doing to it. It's a pity our landlord doesn't live here. His idea of central heating is a candle in the middle of each bedsit.
Ash	It's so cold in winter. We get goose pimples on our goose pimples!
Lara	And ice in our hot water bottles.
Wally	I want to ask you a favour. Could you pass our stuff up to us? It would be a big help.
Lara	Sure. You go on up. There's a light switch just inside the trap door.
Ash	I'm not lifting that heavy vacuum cleaner! I don't want to have a heart attack.
Wayne	I've just lugged it up six lots of stairs!

[*Wally and Wayne go up into the loft*]

Lara	Mind how you go. The loft is full of rubbish left here by past students. Some of it must date back to the time of Florence Nightingale.

Ash	Right, I'll hand things up. Here's this . . . and this . . . and this.
Lara	And here's the vacuum cleaner. Catch!
Wayne	Ouch! Thanks.
Wally	Thanks a lot.
Ash	We'd better go. We've got a lecture.
Lara	More blood and gore. Bye!

[*Lara and Ash leave*]

Wally	Right, Wayne. Listen because this is important. You must only step on the joists. If you step between the joists your foot will go down – through somebody's ceiling. And we don't want that, do we?
Wayne	No . . . oh look! Lots of spiders! They are huge! I don't like spiders!
Wally	Don't shout – you'll hurt their feelings. Now, I think we'll start at this end. Let's move all this rubbish first.
Wayne	Right. [*Clonk*] OUCH!
Wally	I forgot to say – mind your head on the sloping roof. And remember to walk on the joists!
Wayne	It's like walking on a tightrope.
Wally	Come on, help me move this lot. What have we here? Old plaster casts and a pile of splints. Charming!

Wayne	What's this? Funny shape. Someone's written on it in marker pen.
Wally	Let's see what it says. 'BEDPAN: WARD SIX'. Sling it over there.
Wayne	And what can this be?
Wally	It's a footpump – for folk with flat feet.
Wayne	Hey, look at this big tin. [*Shakes tin*] It rattles. I wonder what's in it.
Wally	Well, the label says 'Body Bits'.
Wayne	URRGH! [*Throws tin*]
Wally	Now I just wonder . . .
Wayne	What?
Wally	I just wonder what is under that sheet.
Wayne	I'll have a look. [*He lifts up the sheet*] OH NO! It's a SKELETON! A skeleton without a head!
Wally	Don't get rattled. It's only made of plastic. But I wonder where the head is?
Wayne	I feel all shaky now. [*Clonk*] Ouch! I'm seeing stars!
Wally	I'm going to clean between the joists.

[*He uses the vacuum cleaner, but not for long*]

Wayne	Why has the cleaner stopped?

Wally	It sucked up an old bed sock. I think it's blocked. There's another switch here on the side. I could try that . . .

[*Now the cleaner does not suck – it blows*]

Wayne	Wally! Stop! Look at the mess!
Wally	There. I've switched it off. Now what's the matter?
Wayne	I've just seen another spider. Big as my hand! I've got to get away! [*Clonk*] OUCH!
Wally	Wayne, come out from behind that water tank! A spider can't hurt you.
Wayne	Ow! Ow! Ow!
Wally	What now?
Wayne	I've got my foot stuck.
Wally	How?
Wayne	It's stuck behind a pipe. Stuck fast!
Wally	Hang on. I'll pull you free. There. The shoe is still stuck, but you're free.
Wayne	But now I'll have to work with one bare foot.
Wally	Hard cheese! Now, what's next? Open that roll of glass fibre.
Wayne	Right. That's done. I'll spread it out.
Wally	Funny stuff, isn't it.

Wayne	Yes . . . it's sort of itchy. Ever so itchy! [*Scratching*] Hey, look at my hands – and my arms. All blotchy!

[*Lara and Ash arrive back*]

Lara	[*Calling up into the loft*] Hi, we're back.
Ash	Are you getting on all right?
Wally	[*Looking down from the loft*] I'm all right. But my friend is all blotchy. I hope it's not catching.
Wayne	[*Looking down from the loft*] I was all right until I unrolled the glass fibre.
Lara	Let's have a look. Oh dear. You seem to have a rash.
Ash	It means that your skin is upset. Could be nasty.
Lara	But not fatal. We had a lecture about skin last week.
Ash	Skin is stretchy. Skin is waterproof. Skin holds you together.
Lara	Our lecture today was even better. It was held in the lab. We cut up an eyeball and a pickled lung.
Wayne	DON'T! I feel ill.
Ash	Oh, we love it! Hospital life is great!
Wally	As long as you're not the patient!
Lara	We'd better go. We're off to see our first operation. It should be fun!

Wally	Well, don't laugh – or you'll be in stitches.
Lara	Bye then. Carry on the good work.

[*Lara and Ash leave*]

Wayne	Wally, come here. I can see something weird in this water tank.
Wally	It's the reflection of your face.
Wayne	No, I think it's . . . it's . . . aaaarrgghh! It's a skull! It's the head of the skeleton!
Wally	Chill out, Wayne. It's only plastic.
Wayne	I'm not staying here. [*Clonk*] Ouch!
Wally	Wayne – don't step in between the joists!
Wayne	Oh dear! My foot has gone through.
Wally	Now someone has got a hole in their ceiling! Quick – pull your foot back up!
Wayne	All right. But look. I've lost another shoe. That's two shoes gone. They weren't even mine. They belonged to my brother.
Wally	Don't fuss. Just pack up our things. We've got to get away from here fast.
Wayne	I'm fed up. I've got bumps on my head and blotches on my skin. AND I've got two bare feet!
Wally	Well, you've got a matching pair then! It's like I always say – we're lucky Wally and Co!

Wally and Co: Garden Fixers

4 parts: Wally
          Wayne
          Hector
          Posy

Scene: The large front garden of Hector and Posy Pilkington. Wally and Wayne are about to start work.

Wally	I want this job to go well, Wayne. We might get asked to do other gardens. We could become famous as instant garden fixers. We might be on Ground Force on the telly.
Wayne	I've unpacked the lorry. Wow! We've got loads of stuff!
Wally	Yes, look at it all. Plants in boxes, plants in pots, clumps of flowers, rose bushes, garden tools, a wooden bench, a fountain . . .
Wayne	And even a pair of big iron gates!
Wally	I was lucky to get the load so cheap.
Wayne	Plus the lorry!
Wally	The man in the pub said he wanted a quick sale.

Wayne	But where did he get the stuff?
Wally	I don't know. He just said, 'Ask me no questions and I'll tell you no lies'.
Wayne	That's fair.
Wally	I just wonder why all the little trees have got labels on them.

[*Hector and Posy enter the garden*]

Hector	Good morning, chaps.
Wally	Morning.
Hector	We're very glad to see you.
Posy	Yes, awfully glad.
Hector	We've just moved in here. We don't know a thing about gardening. Not a thing.
Posy	But I know how I want the garden to look. I want it to be private. With a patio.
Hector	We must have a patio.
Posy	And I want roses and a trellis.
Hector	We must have a trellis.
Posy	And I want pots. Lots of pots.
Wally	It's funny that you should want pots. Because we have pots.
Wayne	Lots of pots. No problem.
Posy	What a lot of things you've brought with you.

Wally	You name it – we've got it.
Posy	Oh look! A fountain!
Hector	We saw one like that the other day.
Posy	Yes, it was in the local park.
Hector	Well, chaps, work hard. We're going out now. We want to try out the new Jag.
Posy	We'll see you later. Bye-eee!

[*Hector and Posy leave*]

Wally	Right, Wayne. I want you to dig a row of holes. Then I can bung in these rose bushes. Hurry up. They are wilting.
Wayne	I'm wilting too in this heat. [*He starts to dig*] The ground is as hard as a rock. I think it needs a garden fork.
Wally	Good idea! [*He grabs a fork*] A fork will soon break up the soil.
Wayne	Watch out! OW! OW! OW! Wally, that was my foot!
Wally	It was lucky you had your wellies on.
Wayne	Pah!
Wally	Just keep digging and don't fuss.
Wayne	This is hard work!
Wally	Well, that's that job finished. I feel like a real gardener now.

Wayne   Dig you!

Wally   There – now pop the rose bushes in the holes.

Wayne   Do the roses need a prune?

Wally   No, you're the biggest prune around! Now, our next job is to move the bench. I warn you – it's heavy!

Wayne   Yes . . . [*Straining to lift the bench*] It's very heavy! Let's put it down here. I can't . . . OW! OW! OW! Wally, it's landed on my foot!

Wally   Which foot?

Wayne   Not the one you stabbed with the fork. The other one.

Wally   Well, lucky it was your good foot.

Wayne   I'd kick you, if I could! [*Pause*] Here, look at this brass plate on the bench. It's got writing on it.

Wally   It says, 'In memory of Fred Reeks, late mayor of this town'. I wonder who put that there?

[*Hector and Posy return*]

Hector   I say, you HAVE been busy! [*To Posy*] Look darling, rose bushes all in a row.

Posy   Don't they look a bit . . . dead?

Wally   Don't worry. I'll water them in a minute. They love a drink. They'll soon perk up.

Hector	Oh, how I envy you. You're a real gardener. You know such a lot.
Wally	Tricks of the trade.
Wayne	He knows them all!
Posy	I think our garden will be the best ever.
Hector	I am sure there won't be another one like it.
Wally	I can promise you that.
Posy	We're going out again now.
Hector	We go out a lot.
Posy	We like spending money.
Hector	So we'll be off now. We're going to collect our new Rolls. See you later.
Posy	Work hard. Bye-eee!

[*Hector and Posy leave*]

Wally	I reckon it's time for our lunch break now.
Wayne	Good! All this work and fresh air has made me hungry.

[*Wally and Wayne sit on the bench and start to eat their lunch*]

Wally	Nice bread. I'm going to read the local newspaper. Do you want half?
Wayne	No. I've got my comic. Wally, do spring onions have legs?

Wally   No. Why?

Wayne   I think I've just eaten a caterpillar. Ouch!

Wally   Now what's the matter?

Wayne   I've got a thorn in my finger.

Wally   Take it out then.

Wayne   What? In my lunch break?

[*The garden is quiet, but not for long*]

Wally   NO! I CAN'T BELIEVE IT! I JUST CAN'T BELIEVE IT!

Wayne   What's wrong?

Wally   It says in this newspaper, 'Thieves have stripped the town park bare. They stole trees, shrubs, a fountain and a park bench. They even made off with the park gates! Also missing is the park keeper's lorry'.

Wayne   Well? What has that got to do with us?

Wally   Use your brain, Wayne! The stuff they are talking about is our stuff! All this stuff here in this garden!

Wayne   No!

Wally   Yes! And listen to this! [*Reading*] 'The culprits will be easy to catch. The park gates had just been painted silver'.

[*Wally and Wayne both look at their hands, which are stained with silver paint*]

Wally   Quick! We've got to get away. We can't use that stolen lorry. We'll have to make a run for it.

Wayne   But Wally, how can I run with two bad feet?

Wally   Oh, stop fussing. Do you want a piggy back?

Wayne   Yes. Lucky me!

Wally   Well, that's us. Lucky Wally and Co! Now shut up and run for it!